COCKATOO CAPERS

Cockatoo Capers

Beverly Hoffman Erickson

To order additional copies of this book, contact:
Xlibris Corporation
1-888-795-4274
www.Xlibris.com
Orders@Xlibris.com
59642

CONTENTS

DEDICATION

I would like to dedicate this book to my pet, Todi Cockatoo. She has been a loving pet for almost 30 years. Cockatoos can live to be 100 years old. She is so sweet and has been a wonderful companion hopefully for many more years.

TODI AND QUINCEY

In 1980 in the Spring of the year, we (my former husband, daughter and myself) fell in love with our first larger pet bird, a sulphur crested cockatoo named Todi. Actually we had met Todi a few years before in a local pet shop, named Mr. Friendly.

She stood in the center of the room and seemed strangely attracted to us. She seemed delighted to see us and always let us pet her head.

She had beautiful eyes that sparkled like black marbles and she had blue eye shadow. As a cockatoo she bounced on her perch and she was beautiful.

We answered an ad in the newspaper that read . . . an extremely friendly cockatoo with cage—$700. We discovered it was Todi living at a farm house full of dogs. The owners explained the bird was afraid of the dogs and was frustrated, thus she had plucked out most of her feathers. But she did the disco and also was able to do a somersault if you placed your thumb in back of her back toe. So we took her home with us on a bright Sunday morning mainly due to her personality and the sparkle in her eyes.

I could hear crying in the background as we left with her. I really think the owners didn't really want to sell her.

And it was no wonder. I knew she was some special pet as she was so loving. Being so delighted with her warm personality we felt all cockatoos had this nature.

Naturally we might want to acquire another one so looking in Cage Bird Magazine my husband saw an advertisement, "Large blue eyed Triton cockatoo—male."

We drove into Amish territory in Goshen, Indiana to see the Triton male. When we first saw the bird we felt he was gorgeous. His feathers were perfect, he was very large sitting in a barnyard with other birds.

The owner explained the bird used to be in the house but was moved out to the barn because no one was paying any attention to him. As the bird was being talked about he suddenly flew off his perch. He sailed across the room like an eagle—he was just beautiful even in flight! When he finally circled around and came back he landed on the floor and our then six year old daughter bent down to pick him up. The owner quickly stopped her and explained she would have to use a large leather glove . . . the bird might bite. But she was able to secure him and place him back on his perch.

The Amish farmer gave "Quincey" a soda cracker for safely returning to his perch. Glenn Yoder the owner explained the bird only likes his wife and hated men.

Quincey became another family member for us. The first day home we petted Todi on the head while Quincey watched and he put his foot up to his soft face and started stroking his own chin and head.

When we purchased Todi we were told by the owners that Todi did not like other birds. This now became apparent and she was afraid of Quincey and started to scream at the top of her lungs. Quincey followed suit and we ended up putting the two large birds in separate rooms.

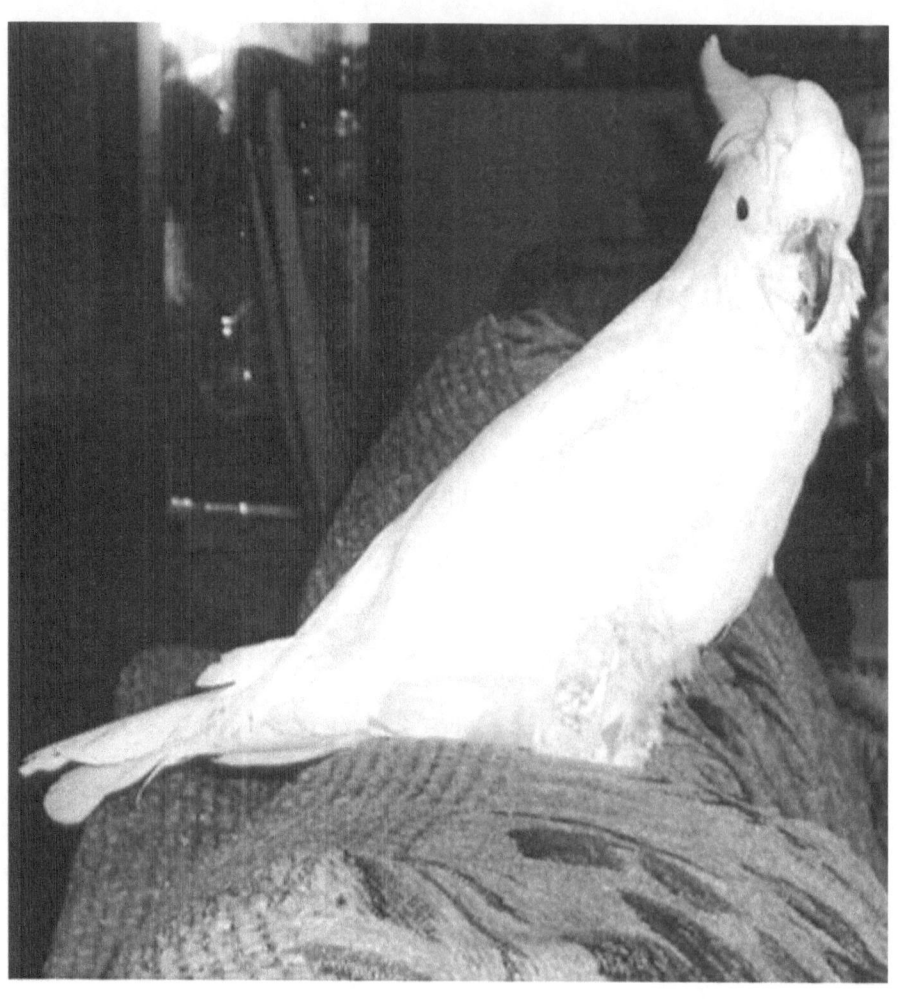

The birds could still see each other and when I'd go up to Quincey's cage to pet him Todi would talk and say, "I feel better Bev. I feel real good!" Well at first I thought she was referring to the state of her health until it became apparent she was saying she felt better to the touch then Quincey.

Todi was right. She did feel better as with Quincey being so moody, I would never know when he might decide to bite. He had large jet black eyes that stood out from his head like marbles. Around his eyes were large blue circles that looked like blue eye shadow. He had a large black beak and very large feet.

His toenails dug into my hand and he had a vice like grip. I begged him to release my hand and his eyes danced in devilment. Slowly he brought my finger to his beak. I asked him, "Does Quincey want a cracker?" He suddenly dropped my finger and proclaimed—"Yes, Quincey wants a cracker!" He had a deep man's voice. I ran to the cupboard and gave him a cracker and he promptly soaked it in his water cup. But he was very polite as he said, "Thank You."

After that incident every morning he would bury his head in his round metal seed cup and start to scream. The screaming would sound louder as it would echo from the metal like a bell. If I didn't respond immediately he would say in a tone of voice that denoted angry "Want cracker now!" As Quincey would say this Todi would softly in her baby girl voice proclaim "I'm better, Bev."

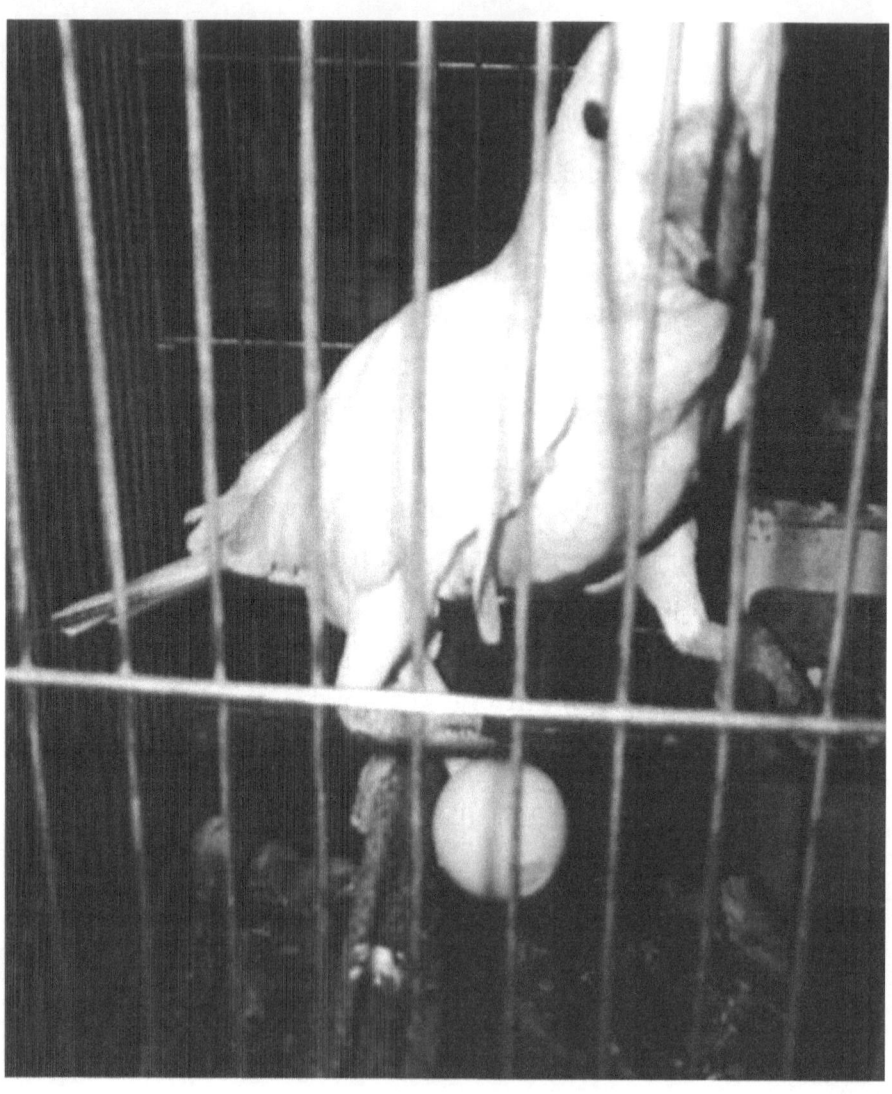

I didn't even have time to get dressed before feeding the birds. Quincey seemed to notice if I was in a night gown as he would stare with another devil like expression. It was apparent he really did like women. Upon placing his seed cup back in his cage he would make a kissing noise.

My former husband started to become restless with this pet. He said, "Can't you stop that big bird from screaming? Maybe we should sell him." At this time Quincey was exercising with his toy dumbbell and he promptly dropped it on the floor of his cage.

When my husband left for work and I walked up to his cage I asked him, "Quincey, why don't you like men?" I really didn't expect a reply but he surprised me and said, "Got batted." I questioned him. "Did this happen when you would scream?" He bowed his head "Yes."

I decided to do some research on cockatoos. The books all said a healthy cockatoo must scream. Also the experts said that the Triton cockatoo was very smart . . . better than other parrots of this species . . . especially the male.

My husband also did some research on Quincey. He discovered Quincey had more than one previous owner. All stated he screamed too much and hated men. Later in life we also learned he killed his mate, so he did not make a good breeder.

One book suggested placing the pet in front of a mirror to suppress the screaming. This I promptly did. Quincey being a very conceited bird loved this, and delighted looking at himself in the mirror for hours. We had to get Todi a mirror too, to try to get her to stop picking out her feathers. For Quincey the screaming seemed to subside for a short while but after the novelty of the mirror wore off he started in again only this time louder. He would stand in front of the mirror and open up his beak and scream in octaves. This way he could watch himself scream.

Our daughter decided to give Quincey singing lessons. She proclaimed, "Maybe Quincey will sing? Maybe he will sing like a canary instead of scream." He loved the music and attention and would bob his head to the beat of the music. One of his favorite songs would be "Let's Get Physical" which Olivia Newton John performed on TV. He'd shout, "Body Talk" at the top of his lungs. Our daughter also discovered Quincey loved to have his picture taken. He would pose for the camera and she'd even dress him in doll clothes to pose for the pictures. This was one trick he had over Todi, as she was afraid of the camera.

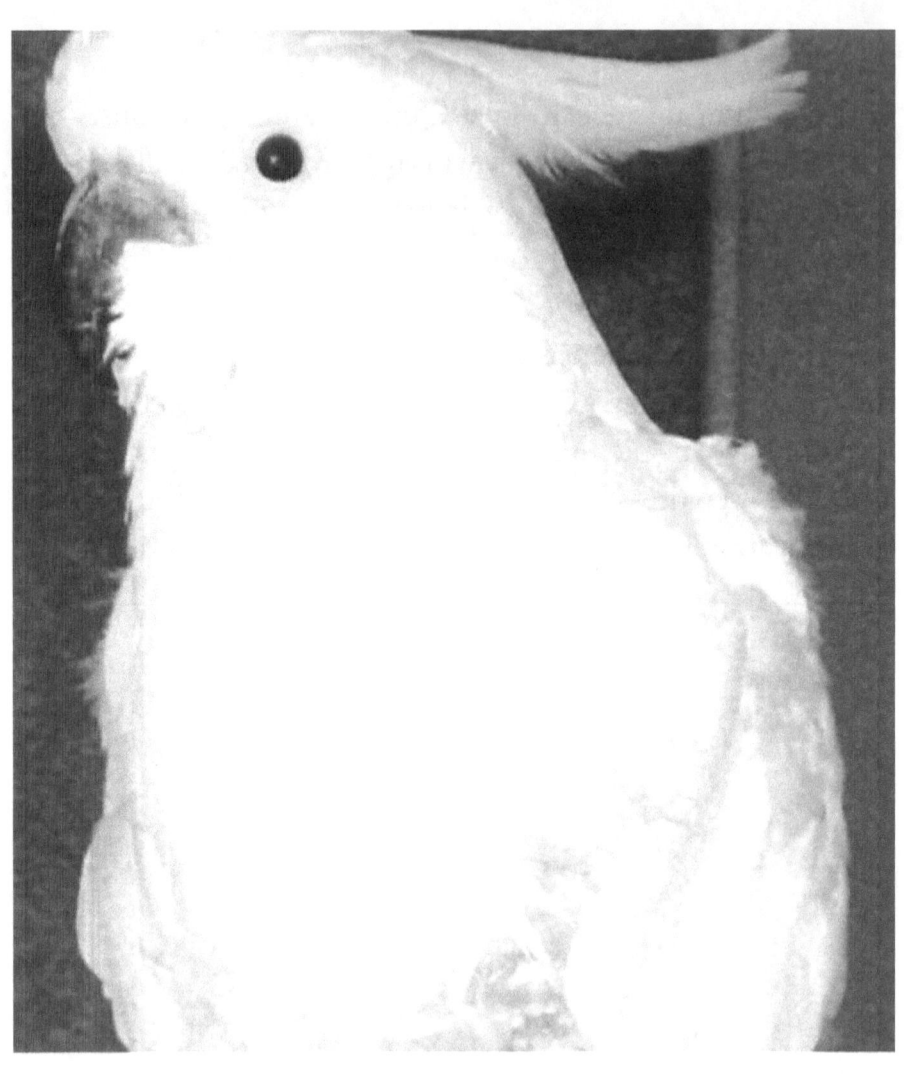

Quincey kept screaming though, and one day my husband looked at Quincey and told him, "You are going to get sold." The next morning both cockatoos were screaming. Quincey stopped and yelled at Todi—"Shutup, get sold."

But the turning point in Quincey's career as a pet came shortly.

At 5:00 a.m. one Sunday morning I lay awake and I heard Todi say "Hi."

Todi's cage was in the dining room by the patio door and Quincey was down the hall by our bedroom. Todi usually never said "Hi" unless she was greeting someone.

I turned to my half awake husband and said, "Why would Todi speak this time of day?

Then suddenly Quincey started to scream. Then both birds started to scream. I waited for both pets to quiet and fell back to sleep.

At 7:00 a.m. when I arose I noticed the patio door was slightly ajar. I walked out on the patio only to notice the garage door opened about half way. I walked back in the house and asked my daughter and husband—"Did you leave the garage door open last night?"

They both said no and walked outside to see. Both noticed Paula's bike was missing.

It was apparent that someone had entered our house at 5:00 A.M. by the dining room and both cockatoos had alarmed the burglar so much he had left in a hurry, probably on the bike.

Now Quincey was a hero. He had alerted our other pet bird to sound an alarm. He was given a special treat that day and my husband went out and bought him a new cage. It was apparent that he was to become a permanent resident in our home.

A Trip to the Bird Show

Everyone dreams of entering their pet in a bird contest and coming in first place. We felt Quincey Vincent, a cockatoo, was a first place bird. After all he stood tall and erect, was of perfect feather and liked to show off his crest.

Well, here's what happened. We put him in a little dog kennel and packed him in the back seat of our car. We drove in the country on the way to Ft. Wayne, Indiana on a crisp October day. All the way riding his eyes were watering and he suddenly got sick to his stomach. We thought he was only excited or had eaten old seed.

When we arrived we put him in his cage and gave him a plant spray shower since he loved water. He usually would hold his wings out wide as the water sprayed on him. To our amazement he just stood there and let the water roll off him like a duck. His tongue was hanging out and he was panting. We felt surely he would adjust by the next morning. All the other birds were settling down to sleep. We covered Quincey's cage so he would not catch cold.

The next morning he appeared worse, he had not eaten any of his favorite seeds and he hung his head. His feathers were still wet from the night before and he held his wings strangely like they were broken. He stared at all the strangers and hissed. No one would have guessed he wasn't completely wild or would ever talk. Someone commented, "Who brought that ugly parrot?"

When it came time for the judge to see him he hung his head and looked away. All the other cockatoos performed well and seemed alert. One proud white bird even fanned out his tail feathers as the judge pointed his marker at him. Quincey even watched this bird not impressed at all. The other parrot seemed to be trying to get our pet's attention. Perhaps the bird's extreme confidence made our pet feel inferior? Never-the-less Quincey was not interested.

The judge came to Quincey's cage. I heard him say to the other judge, "What is wrong here? Is this bird's wing broken, he holds it out so stiff? Look at that posture, he is standing very stooped. His feathers are matted looking." Meanwhile Quincey's eyes kept watering like he had a terrible cold. He came in third place among three cockatoos.

He didn't perk up until time to go home, putting him back in the dog kennel he snuggled up and we could pet him all over. I asked him if he thought he was being sold and he bobbed his head, "Yes."

All the way home he purred like a kitten. He still would not eat any of his seed when offered it though.

The minute we arrived back home and walked in the living room, I opened up the dog carrier he was in. He quickly flew out and headed for his bedroom and climbed in his cage. I walked in the room and he quickly pulled his own cage door shut. Normally he was eager to get out of his cage. I showed him the small white third place ribbon he had won. I told him that he could have done better because he is such a beautiful bird. He glanced over at the mirror and slowly spread his tail feathers out and stood tall again.

I left the room and when I came back he was eating his seed and playing with his favorite toy, a baby dumbbell. I asked him again, "Why didn't he perform like the other birds and make us proud?" He quickly dropped his toy dumbbell on the floor and gave me a cold hard stare.

After a few strained moments I told him we would never take him to a show again. He stood tall again and spoke one word, "Good!"